Balcony, patio and window box gardening

Leslie Johns

Edited for U.S. Gardeners
By Marjorie Dietz

Floraprint

Published 1977 by Floraprint Limited,
Park Road, Calverton, Nottingham.
Designed and produced for Floraprint by
Intercontinental Book Productions
Copyright © 1977 Intercontinental Book Productions
and Floraprint Limited. North American edition
Copyright© 1981 Intercontinental Book Productions and
Floraprint U.S.A.

ISBN 0-938804-03-0

Design by Design Practitioners Limited

Photographs supplied by Floraprint Limited (copyright
I.G.A.), Leslie Johns and Associates, Harry Smith, Kenneth
Scowen

Printed in U.S.A.

Contents

1 The pros and cons of container gardening

Diversity makes this patio a place of interest in all seasons, yet there is space left which is open and uncluttered.

Some people whose gardening activities are restricted to filling a few pots on a balcony, a few tubs on a patio or a roof, or to tending a window box might feel that they are underprivileged gardeners, deprived of their right to get their fingers into the real soil, to get mud on their boots and thorns in their fingers. But they would be very wrong.

This type of gardening could with advantage be called container gardening, for it must be carried out almost entirely in containers rather than in mother earth. Con-tainer gardening is probably the easiest most rewarding, most exciting and mos foolproof type of gardening there can be, fo the gardener is in complete control ove everything except the weather, and even this he can command to a certain extent.

The gardener can choose his own con-tainers, their size, shape, color, material He can decide where they are to be placed in this corner or that, at this height or that

4

He can decide what kind of soil he will put in them, sandy or peaty, acid or alkaline, heavy or light. He can decide which plants he wishes to grow and even though his residence may be in a belt of the most uncompromising lime, he can grow in his containers fine plants of rhododendrons, azaleas and ericas. He can change his display at will, moving his containers from place to place or emptying them according to season and replacing their contents with fresher, more colorful plants. If frosts come, he can even bring a container into the home for a night, or two, or place it where it will otherwise receive some shelter. He can plant spring-flowering bulbs in his containers at the end of the summer and overplant these with ericas, happy in the knowledge that he will have a certain amount of winter color and all the promise of a glorious spring, yet during the colder and darker months he need never step out onto his balcony, say, to tend his plants, for they will look after themselves.

What limitations, then, face the container gardener? What problems will he find? In the first place it will be apparent that he is limited by size. Almost any plant,

Geraniums (pelargoniums) provide vivid colorful bloom over a long period.

Contrast of color and shape on this balcony ensures a peaceful beauty with minimum attention

even trees of considerable size, can be grown in a container so long as it is large enough. But one cannot grow a tree in a window box, nor on most balconies, unless it be either one that can be kept under strict control – such as a clipped bay tree – or perhaps one of the dwarfed bonsai trees. The gardener is also limited by weight, for a container filled with moist soil can be heavy indeed, certainly too heavy to move about with ease, and sometimes too heavy structurally. There is, then, a tendency for gardeners to choose fairly small containers made from some lightweight material (rather than stone, concrete or other durable but heavy material) for the sake of convenience.

The fact that the containers used are mainly on the small side presents another problem, for small containers dry out very quickly and in warm or dry weather can require watering twice a day. This can be an awkward chore and a considerable tie, for it may mean that one is unable to go away for a weekend, for example, without making arrangements for the plants to be watered or without installing some automatic watering device.

But these are comparatively minor problems when one considers that no heavy digging, no constant weeding, no regular mowing of the lawn, no hedge trimming, and no carting away of piles of garden refuse are involved.

Although the three types of gardening mentioned here have been grouped together under the title of container gardening, certain minor differences exist, owing mainly to physical conditions. The balcony is larger than a window box, but probably smaller than the patio. So let us have a brief look at each of these locations.

Balcony gardens

With a balcony one must make up one's mind right at the beginning whether the

The use of masses of vivid color in containers is well-suited to hot and sunny climates.

Where the sun is strong the gardener seeks shade, but flowers will grow and cover themselves with bloom, delighting the eye with their decoration.

garden is to be for the benefit of the residents or for the pleasure of passers-by. Are the plants to be enjoyed from indoors or are they to be placed on the exterior of the building so that they are hardly seen from indoors? A balcony is almost always bounded by a wall or a balustrade of some kind. Plants in their pots can be placed against this so as to leave as much room as possible, or they can be hung or otherwise fastened to the outside of the wall or railing. If both locations are used – growing plants on the balcony for the benefit of those indoors and at the same time *outside* the balustrade for the benefit of strangers – there will be problems of handling, reaching and stretching. There will also be problems of watering and the danger of debris falling into premises below or onto the street, something that must always be avoided.

On the whole it is probably better to create the balcony garden so that it can be seen at its best by the residents of the apartment. By using raised boxes, hanging baskets and the like there will be every opportunity of adding to the decoration of the building and the district at the same time.

There are several little problems that will face the new balcony gardener. For example, until one has experienced living high

A variety of containers: *from left,* an evocative urn; a classic trough; a coopered half-barrel; a shallow saucer; and a terra-cotta jar with planting holes.

7

above street level it is impossible to imagine how much more wind there is, not only in quantity and strength, but – more important – in unpredictability. One never knows from which direction it will arrive, regardless of prevailing winds. So it is vital to take this wind into account. In certain positions a hanging basket may swing so violently in the wind as to be a positive danger, yet moved further back or against a wall it may do no more than rock gently in the breeze. Dry soil or peat moss may be blown away and a jet of water from a hose can easily find its way into a neighbor's windows. Plants usually have to be well-staked or otherwise supported. Better still, they should be comparatively dwarf so they will not snap off or rock in their pots.

Another problem that can face the balcony gardener concerns the sun. Some balconies can be in full sun for almost the entire day, others can be so affected by shade that certain plants just cannot be grown successfully. There is nothing that can be done about this other than adapting one's style of gardening to the existing conditions.

There is also the question of weight. A box of pansies bought from a street market may weigh only a few pounds, but once they have been removed and planted in several pots or troughs of soil the total weight will have increased considerably, and when freshly watered they will be even heavier. Although this extra weight will not affect the structural safety of your balcony,

A built-in tray prevents problems with drips when hanging baskets are being watered.

you may find that if you have to move pots or tubs, they may be heavier than you can conveniently manage; and if they are to be lifted above floor level and fixed in position, you may find that soil and plants have to be removed first.

Debris can be a nuisance on a balcony. Dust and soil crumbs, fallen leaves, dead flowers, a broken pot, seed packets and labels – all these can be a nuisance, disfiguring an otherwise pleasant scene if they are allowed to blow about in the wind. For this reason it is always wise and helpful to maintain a covered trash can into which rubbish can be placed at the first opportunity so that the place is kept clean and tidy and so there is no likelihood of annoying neighbors.

Plants growing on a balcony should normally be in containers with drainage holes in them, although if they can be protected from rain this is not essential. Drainage holes will allow water to trickle through and onto the floor. However, this water can stain some surfaces, and it may linger in puddles and become a nuisance. Again, the copious watering needed at some times of the year means that fertilizers are constantly leached from the soil and require

Wooden window boxes are long-lasting, and a metal tray underneath will catch excess water.

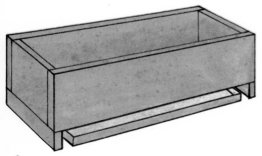

replacing. For all these reasons it is helpful to stand pots on the balcony inside a saucer or some other container or to fit drip trays underneath them to catch and contain any excess water. This can then be returned to the plant soil at the next watering and will help to reduce the fertilizer bill.

Window boxes

Window boxes offer rather less opportunity for gardening than the space of a balcony. They also offer additional problems, the greatest and most important of which concerns the actual box or container and the way in which it is fixed in position. There can be no half measures with window boxes; they must be sound and undamaged, they must be securely held in their positions and they must have means for the collection of excess water or for its safe removal. This water must not be allowed to drip down into the street because of the damage or danger it might cause.

There are restrictive clauses in the leases of some city buildings prohibiting window boxes and it is worth checking this out before installing any. Insurance policies should be examined, for if you are not covered for any possible damage or injury you could be open to heavy costs. It is therefore only prudent to make sure that if you do install window boxes they should both fit the windows for which they are intended and they should be securely fixed in place so that they cannot possibly fall.

It is this necessity for careful fixing that has led to the use of timber almost exclusively for the construction of window boxes, for this is a material that is easy to cut to size and easy to fix to walls or windowsills. The timber should be sound and not less than 1 in (25–30 mm) thick, and it should be well preserved with several coats of paint. The window box should be not less than 6 in (15 cm) deep and wide, preferably more. If possible, it should be fixed in position slightly above the actual sill so that a removable drip pan can be placed underneath it to catch any excess water. This should be of metal, and, once again, it should be either fixed in position or so secure that no wind or casual knock can send it

When constructing a window box, you should try to include the useful features shown here. The wood should be heavy and drilled for drainage. It should fit the space closely and safely, yet allow room at the sides for picking it up, and underneath for a drip tray.

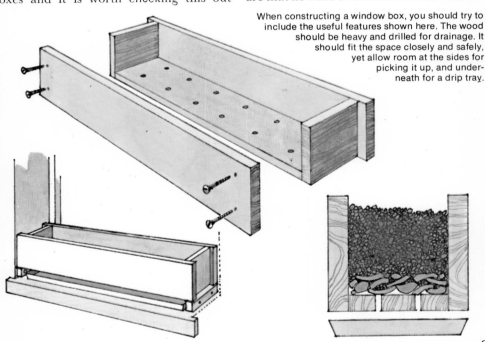

9

falling to the street below; yet it should be easily removed and replaced from inside the room, rather than being accessible only by means of a ladder in the front of the building.

A filled window box can be very heavy, so it is essential to fix it in position empty, and then fill it. It should have drainage holes in the base and there should be a drainage layer on the floor at least 1 in (2–3 cm) deep, with the soil above this. The soil mixture should be rich and well drained, yet with sufficient peat to hold moisture well. Too much peat or a soilless compost will almost certainly mean moisture loss by wind erosion.

Do not attempt to sow seeds in a window box, for uneven temperatures and the almost inevitable occasional dryness will inhibit their germination. Grow your plants indoors and then plant them out or buy ready-grown plants. Make sure that they are always at their best, for a shabby window box with half-dead plants is an eyesore. Any plant past its best should be removed and replaced.

Above: Window boxes need not be empty in winter. Evergreens such as English ivy, aucuba, ericas and skimmia can be underplanted with dwarf spring-flowering bulbs like crocuses, daffodils and tulips.

Below: Zinnias, mesembryanthemums and geraniums will flourish in a window box in hot sun if they are watered regularly.

Above: Where shade is a problem for part of the day, pansies can be persuaded to flower in spring and can be followed by wax begonias and calceolaria.

Keep window boxes going in winter as well as in summer. Use evergreens such as skimmia, winter-flowering ericas or heaths and ivy, dwarf conifers, possibly under-planted with spring-flowering bulbs. Choose dwarf varieties of daffodils and tulips, as well as smaller bulbs such as crocus and grape-hyacinth, for tall-stemmed kinds will almost certainly snap in the wind.

In summer the plants you grow will depend largely on whether the site is mainly in the sun or the shade. In the first condition use nasturtium, French marigolds, zinnias, and the always useful geraniums. If shade is a problem, try *Vinca rosea*, begonias and impatiens.

Patios and terraces

A patio or terrace is less likely to present shade problems, unless it conforms to the narrow definition of this site as a courtyard completely surrounded by buildings. The name has come to mean what is almost an outdoor room attached to the house, frequently linking the house and the garden,

11

lying as it does between the two. It has also come to mean the backyard of a town house, an area too small to be labeled a garden and probably paved overall, with perhaps a few gaps in which plants are grown. But having considerably more space than is available either on a balcony or in a window box, shaded parts of the patio can be used for shade plants and the sunnier portion filled with sun-loving plants. It is also possible to use light-colored paints to cover some or all of the walls, which will considerably increase the intensity of the available light.

Patio gardening gives the best of all worlds, for it makes it possible to plant some material directly in the soil, yet it also encourages the use of containers. The containers can be large and weighty. There is no need to worry about drips of excess water from any containers. Some plantings can be on a semi-permanent basis, while others can be as temporary as desired.

Unless one inherits a patio that has been used with intelligence and thoroughness, it is probable that the soil on the site will be cold, thin, sour and unproductive, so it will be well worth digging out the top layer where you intend to plant, and replacing it with some fresh and healthy loam. It is easy

enough to replace the soil in containers of growing plants, except where the containers are built-in or permanent structures, which might be more difficult.

Only in the most fortunate of conditions can a patio be made to look like a garden or even made into a green and pleasant retreat from the world. As a general rule, one cannot escape from a certain formality, from straight lines, from flat paving, from a built-in and slightly claustrophobic atmosphere. Yet on these bases it is perfectly possible to build an outdoor room of charm and beauty, to disguise the straight lines, conceal the flatness, and soften the surrounding walls with green growth.

It may be that the patio has to hold such unsightly objects as an oil tank or a trash can. It will probably have a pile of soil and perhaps some sand or a bale or two of peat moss, some tools and a roll of hose pipe. The thing to do is to build the patio in such a manner that these necessities can be concealed, yet readily available for use at any time. This is not a difficult thing to do so long as it is done right at the beginning and the work is carried out with the overall

'Before': It would seem impossible to transform this small, enclosed, obstructed place into a spacious and elegant garden.

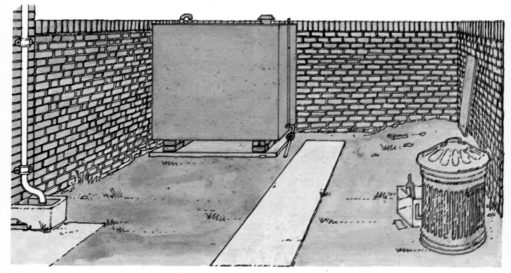

'After': Tank and trash can are hidden; the wall is lightened and heightened; and paving, plants and containers have been selected with care.

appearance in mind. A light screen can cover the oil tank, for example, with a rampant *Polygonum baldschuanicum* (silver lace vine, also listed as *P. aubertii*) growing on and through it, the plant's tendrils and creamy flowers concealing the functional interior. Seats with removable lids can hold tools. A wall with a built-in flower strip along the top can have concealed in its belly a cavity that will hold a good sack of soil. All this is a matter of good design and imagination, and where space is so limited it is essential that every square of it should be used both to give pleasure and to ease normal house and garden-keeping. If the patio is made into an exquisite retreat from life at the expense of comfort in the home, or if it becomes unrealistic in its demands for constant clearing, it will be more of an irritation than a pleasure.

Planting in soil If the area has been paved overall and you want to make certain plantings direct into the soil, it will probably be possible without too much trouble to remove one or two paving slabs here and there. The soil beneath is certain to be poor and unproductive, so it should be removed to a depth of at least 6 in (15 cm) and more if this is not too difficult. In order to check that drainage will be sufficient or suitable, pour a bucket or two of water into the hole just excavated to make sure that it runs away satisfactorily. If the drainage is poor

13

and the water lies in the hole for more than a very few minutes, it will become necessary to dig out more soil and to break up the subsoil.

Fill the hole with fresh soil according to what you intend to plant. If you have in mind a small tree or a shrub, then fill the hole with a soil mixture that will provide nourishment to the plant over a long period. Place in the bottom of the hole a spadeful of well-rotted farmyard manure, if you can get it, and mix a few handfuls of peat with your loam or leafmold, which you sift in around the roots of your tree. Firm the soil well around the roots and then cover the naked soil with pebbles or something similar to give the finishing touch of

A pavement planting such as this should be bursting with plants, packed tightly so no soil shows through. This means a rich, well-fed soil, regular watering and constant dead-heading of the flowers.

smartness and to keep soil off the paving.

If you intend to grow something more brightly colored and cheerful, such as a little rectangle of vivid annuals, then plant these in a soil and peat mixture, about half and half, which has been well enriched with a slow-acting fertilizer, perhaps bonemeal or one of the proprietary types available. Make sure that the little patch is watered regularly and that all dead flowers are removed as soon as they begin to look faded. This will ensure that the bed always looks neat and it will help the production of further blooms.

When winter comes, the occupants of this summer bed will have to be removed and one is then left with a vacant space. It can be filled with some hardy material, such as heathers or ivy, but one cannot continually be lifting and planting in this manner, so a possible answer to this winter problem is merely to replace the original paving. This need not be done with any great thoroughness, for it will be a temporary measure, but it will help to disguise the vacant space until the spring comes around again.

Herb gardens It is possible on a patio to grow a few of the most useful herbs for the kitchen. Some can be grown in pots but, if there is space, most will do better in the soil. A tiny section can be marked out like a chess board and different herbs grown in each of the squares. In this way you can also help to provide the type of soil enjoyed by the different herbs, a deep, rich loam for the apple mint, a well-drained sandy soil for a little sage bush and so on. Some of the herbs will quickly outgrow the small space allotted to them, so use cuttings to replace a plant that has grown too large for its square, or continue to sow fast-growing herbs such as chervil, dill, or basil.

Raised beds Consider also making a herb garden on a raised bed at waist height, although lower beds, 12 in (30 cm) or 18 in (45 cm) high, the last permitting the gar-

A raised bed like this allows fragrant, colorful flowers and plants to be enjoyed with utmost ease.

dener to perch on the edge as he works, are also practical, and easier to build. Raised beds are useful for several reasons and they can give vast pleasure because the plants grow almost at nose level so one can pinch and smell easily. Waist-high gardening is also ideal for those who through age, accident or illness cannot bend to do their gardening at ground level. At this height they can plant and weed from a chair or even from a wheelchair, or they can stand, using a cane, to pluck out an invasive weed. In some cases the incapacitated can even perch on the broad side of an elevated garden and carry out simple operations from that position.

This last suggestion presupposes not so much a raised container as one that is built into a raised portion of the patio – in effect where there are two walls with an interior trough, usually planted up with bright plants to make a colorful band along the top of the wall. The actual soil container is seldom more than about 1 ft (30 cm) deep and this rests on top of the otherwise solid or core-packed wall.

If a flower bed is to be raised to waist level, then it must be quite secure and there must be no danger that the sides will crumble and give way. For this reason the building of raised beds can be a somewhat lengthy business unless you choose the lower heights mentioned above. Even with a raised bed only 16–18 in (40–45 cm) high, it will be necessary to construct it carefully. One of the easiest materials to use today are railroad ties, which measure about 10 in (24 cm) high and about 8 in (20 cm) wide. However, railroad ties are heavy, bulky and difficult to cut apart without power saws, although most lumber yards and some garden centers can help here once you have determined your dimensions. Much easier to handle and cut apart are the lighter, smaller 'landscape' ties, now carried by most lumber yards. They measure about 4 by 4 in (10 by 10 cm) and make handsome, long-lasting walls, edging, and steps.

An attractive raised bed results if the walls are made from natural or reconstituted stone, although this is a more lengthy process, normally requiring a concrete foundation for the considerable weight of the stones.

Raised beds can also be made with strips of boards, cement blocks or, for a more formal effect, bricks. The last will require cement to hold them securely, as well as some skill to construct. Prefabricated patio blocks might be used, but their dimensions are more suited to paving uses, and to make a raised bed of much height would require many, many blocks.

Once the dimensions of the bed have been decided and the ties or boards cut to proper lengths, the ground should be excavated to about 6–8 in (15–20 cm) deep of this size. The ties or boards can then be placed around the perimeter, outside the excavated area, which should be filled with pieces of broken pots, bricks, stones, pebbles, coarse coal ashes or whatever material is available as filling and draining matter.

The remaining space can then be filled with soil, preferably after placing some sealing material on top of the rubble to prevent the soil from trickling down too far. The type of soil used will depend on what is to be grown, and even more on what is available. City dwellers don't have much choice – the usual soil found in cities differing widely in quality and type. A big help are the soilless mixes, available under different trade names as Jiffy Mix, Redi Earth, Pro-Mix, Super Soil. These soilless mixes can be added to soils in varying proportions, and should greatly improve their moisture-holding capacity.

A raised bed is easily made with regular paving slabs, which because they are strong and slim allow large areas of soil to be used. Natural stone walls are attractive but need a foundation and greater space.

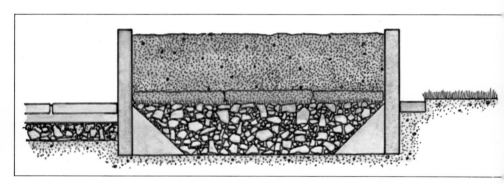

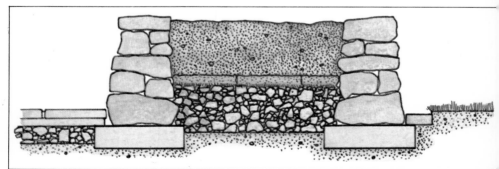

Peat bricks, occasionally used abroad, should be thoroughly soaked in water before being used to make a retaining wall. This makes them more stable and workable.

Electricity on the patio Try always to bear in mind the fact that a patio is an extension of the house, an outdoor room meant to be lived in, to be used and occupied. If you remove your furniture rather than leave it on the patio at all times and in all seasons, then make it easy to get out so that you waste no time and do not find it too much of a chore. Eat out of doors whenever weather encourages this activity. Install lighting, its type depending on the area available, but always bear in mind that glaring, overall flood-lighting will annoy or disconcert neighbors and will certainly not be attractive to anyone sitting out in it. It is far better to use just two or three smaller lighting units concealed among your plants, so that they are highlighted. At the same time you have a useful but not obtrusive lighting of certain parts of the patio while other parts are kept dim and mysterious.

If you are going to install exterior lighting on the patio, make sure that your electrical wiring is both safe and unobtrusive. Engage the services of a competent electrician if you are not sure of what you are doing. You can either install a permanent system of electricity with one or two basic outlets into which you can plug your electric lights as and when you wish to use them, or, you can merely drape electric cable along the garden from the house for use on special occasions and remove it again at the earliest convenient time.

A permanent system will probably leave the house and travel through the garden to the required spots in a specially armored and insulated cable, which is expensive but safe and long-lasting. If a spade should accidentally descend upon cable of this type, it will do no damage. The outlets it is connected to would be of a special water and weatherproof type, suitable under all conditions.

In fact, the possibilities open to exploitation by the possession of a patio are limited only by the amount of money and time available, and it has been known for a patio to be changed into a conservatory by the erection of a glass roof over the area, as the ultimate in garden luxury.

2 Containers

Materials

Above: Containers are available in a wide variety of shapes and a large choice of materials.

Under normal gardening conditions, when plants are grown in pots or containers of any kind, these look best if they have some affinity with the soil – that is, if they are of stone, clay, terra-cotta, wood, even metal. But gardening on a balcony, on a patio or in a window box is not normal gardening and this fact enormously widens the list of materials that are available for use as containers in these places.

Stone and concrete Stone flower containers are often prohibitively priced. They must be made by hand and, consequently, they are seldom produced today. Old models come from antique shops with price tags suggesting that the stone used is precious rather than mundane. Fortunately, the problem has been recognized and is being rectified by the use of reconstituted stone.

Its main virtue is that it can be molded, which means that many copies of a single model can be made instead of just one. Inevitably, this leads to a limited number of designs and the fact that one is likely to see one's own containers in a neighbor's garden, but this matters less today than it used to do. Designs are chosen that have a universal appeal and will suit most surroundings and conditions, and it is from these that the artificial stone duplicates are made. Sometimes they tend to be somewhat grainy, crumbly and soft at first, but normal weathering can be expected to harden and mature them so that they become safe under conditions of normal handling. Harder and tougher are those models that are cast in concrete rather than molded in stone; when new, these seem to have a somewhat unsympathetic surface texture, yet this again weathers to become a great deal more appealing.

Above: Unusual containers always appeal, but they should be practical enough to hold sufficient soil.

Below: Terra-cotta is used for all these containers.

All stone and concrete containers by the nature of the material are bound to be somewhat large and heavy, an impressive addition to patio design. They need to be placed carefully and are often improved if stood on a plinth or formal base. Various plinths, bases and balustrades are also available in reconstituted stone, as indeed are a range of statuary and ornaments that do much to bring back into the garden or even the patio a grace of decoration that was for a time lost because of the expense.

Asbestos A material similar in some respects to stone but lighter in weight and thinner in section is asbestos, used to produce containers that are pleasant in shape, comparatively light in weight, neutral in color and flexible in design. Being thinner,

Left: Half-sphere containers such as this are often available at reasonable cost.
Below: New shapes and materials are constantly being produced for the patio or terrace.

this material is particularly suitable for making smaller containers.

Wood The most common material for a window box is wood, and wood (redwood, cypress and others) is commonly used for tubs, square or rectangular planters and raised beds. This is because a wooden box can be made exactly to measure and, in the case of a window box, can be fixed in position with brackets or screws without trouble. If using wood, make sure that it is stout enough to last for more than one or two seasons. It should normally be at least 1 in (2–3 cm) thick and of a dense timber such as redwood. The exterior will probably be painted, but before this is done the entire surface should be coated inside and out with one of the copper naphthenate solutions, normally available as solutions in green, brown or natural. Do not use creosote, which is toxic to plants until it is old. If the box is painted, make sure that the paint has dried and all fumes have dissipated before doing any planting. The copper naphthenate solution will add years to

21

Above: Choose containers to fit the style of the plant and the atmosphere of the site. *Below*: Always conceal the mouths of containers like this with plant growth.

the life of wood because it inhibits attack by all fungi and many insects.

Plastic and fiberglass Various types of plastic substances have been used for the production of containers, from the traditional flower pot to larger and more elaborate designs. Few of these plastic containers are suitable for window box use, mainly because of their lightness in weight and the fact that they are not easy to fix permanently and safely in position. A stronger material than most plastic is glass fiber, and apart from the fact that this again is dangerously light in weight, a fiberglass window box can generally be fixed securely in position. Fiberglass can be made in the widest possible range of shapes and designs, and finishes can also be controlled to some extent so that the completed container can look like plastic, timber or, most successfully, like antique lead. Fiberglass is not as cheap as most plastic, but, on the other hand, it is virtually everlasting, whereas some of the less expensive plastics tend to degrade under the influence of sunlight and lose their color and strength so that eventually they begin to split and must be replaced.

Choosing containers

Containers should be chosen carefully, partly for their suitability to the task and partly for aesthetic reasons. A little imagination and knowledge of what's available can be the keys to proper container acquisition. Antique and second-hand shops don't just offer expensive stoneware. Sometimes quite reasonable discarded farm feeding troughs can be found, or weathered wooden barrels can turn up. Don't overlook possibilities in pottery studies, where often not-so-costly ceramic containers are sold. Then there are also the prosaic tin cans,

Above: This plastic container is in the style of a coopered timber tub but is longer lasting.
Below: A few potted plants and a climber or two will quickly furnish an otherwise stark patio.

23

Where a container is unlikely to be moved, it can be as large as you like and hold anything up to a tree.

all containers have to be first transported to the spot where they are to be filled. This again suggests that, to say the least, lightness will be a convenience.

Clean colors suit balcony use because they fit into any decorative scheme. Plastic surfaces can easily be kept clean, wiped down quickly with a damp cloth or sponge. Some plastic surfaces will accept the growth of algae, molds and moss unless they are cleaned regularly. This may not be of importance in a garden or even on occasion on some patios, but, as a general rule, a soiled container like this would not be acceptable on a balcony.

Because a balcony is normally smaller than a patio it cannot accommodate the cumbersome containers of large plants that might be appropriate for the patio. So to get the same effect of flower and plant color on the balcony, one is forced to use a greater number of containers. There is nothing wrong with this so long as they are mainly massed together and not dotted about piecemeal. On a patio it is possible to cover an entire wall with a single plant growing either in the soil or in a large container. As far as the balcony is concerned neither the wall space nor the large container is available, so for concentrated impact a large number of pots must be massed together, some raised or banked to be easily visible.

Containers for growing crops

The plants grown on a balcony, in a window box or on a patio are nearly always purely decorative. The exception might be a few herbs grown on the patio. This is traditional, but there are a number of other, less traditional crops that are now being grown in these locations. Examples include lettuce, carrots, cress, Swiss chard, and mustard, which grow best in window boxes or planters. In tubs, large pots, even bushel baskets, grow tomatoes, eggplant, pepper and cucumber.

In comparatively recent years a new method of growing some of these crops has been developed in England and is just

discards from the kitchen. These can be sprayed with paint, punched with drainage holes, and used as hanging or stationary containers.

In addition, on a charming and sophisticated town patio, plastic containers would seem to strike a wrong note unless the design is also sophisticated. But plastic on a balcony seems much more at home, probably because it is functionally correct in its lightness and its easily cleaned surfaces. The balcony is more an extension of the house than is the patio, for it is connected to the home, whereas the patio proper is a link with house and with garden.

On a balcony it is almost certain that a container of growing plants will have to be moved on occasion. This means that it must be as light in weight as possible. One should also remember, when buying, that

advisable to use the bag for a second crop.)

It is a clean, easy and efficient way of growing, and one eminently suited to use on the patio or the balcony. The sacks are not, perhaps, attractive in appearance, but they can be disguised or hidden and it is, after all, the crop that is most important.

Hanging baskets

Hanging baskets are a useful and charming addition to a balcony display and they can

Left and below: Why empty the growing medium out of the sack into a container if you can use the bag itself as the container? These growing bags are used mainly for the convenient culture of vegetables and salads.

beginning to catch on in the United States, a method that for various reasons has proved so successful that it has been widely adopted by the commercial growing world, which we can accept as an indication of its viability. Basically, the idea is that instead of buying a special soil mixture and scooping this out of its sack into containers, the sack itself is used as the container. It is laid flat on the floor, and is slit open. Then the crop, such as tomato plants, for example, are placed in it just as they might be in a clay pot or in soil.

The plastic sack, sometimes called a 'pillow pak', is waterproof and the growing medium, normally a specially enriched peat mixture, is clean, sterile and balanced. All that is needed is the addition of water. Although these growing bags appear to be expensive and make the cost of the tomatoes or lettuce grown in them no cheaper than those in the shops, they are highly convenient and easy to use, and the growing medium can subsequently be used in the garden or to fill other pots. (It is not

provide color high on a wall, helping to make the most of the limited space available. They are unusual decorations, which bring welcome splashes of color where they are not normally expected.

The usual type of frame for a hanging basket is a half sphere of galvanized wire 12–18 in (30–45 cm) in diameter and provided with chains and a ring for hanging.

There are also types, usually made from some plastic material, which involve fewer problems. In either case the bracket from which the basket is to be hung must be strong and firmly fixed to the wall, for the basket, when planted and watered, can be very heavy indeed. Although they should be placed high enough to be out of the way of people walking below, they should not be so high that they are difficult to water, for they dry out quickly and will require water both morning and evening on a dry and sunny day. Make sure that any drips that might fall cannot harm other plants that are growing below, and, if the baskets are in a position over a street or sidewalk, see that they are hung so as not to drip on unwary passers-by.

When you are using a wire frame basket, it must have a lining to serve as a cup or container for the soil. Moss is the best material for this, but as this is not always available or easy to obtain, other materials will suffice. Thin sods of grass, laid so that the grass is on the inside and the soil on the outside, will be a useful substitute if you have access to them. Alternatively, pieces of burlap will usually last for a season and, if it is coarse enough, will allow shoots of some plants to grow through it and so clothe the basket in growing green, for the purpose will be to have flowers and foliage everywhere. Some wire and plastic baskets now come with a molded fiber liner. And it is possible to line the basket with plastic

sheeting, but remember that holes must be made in the bottom to permit excess water to escape.

Having lined the wire basket, fill the interior with a good, rich soil. Knock the plants from their pots and plant them in this compost, positioning them to trail prettily over the edges or even to grow downwards through the lining. Water the basket thoroughly and make sure that it is never allowed to dry out. You will find that on some days this will mean watering twice or even three times, so it may be worth your while to fix a hose on to a cane so that it can be lifted easily, to water from a window above or to have the hanging basket on a rope and pulley so that it can easily be lowered. In the last case it will sometimes be helpful to water the basket by immersion rather than by pouring water from above. Simply drop it into a bucket or basin and leave it there until uniformly moist, then allow to drain and restore it to its correct position.

Plastic hanging baskets will not normally allow plants to grow through the base, so it is more than ever necessary to have plants or trails hanging over the sides so as to conceal what might otherwise be a rather ugly naked material. On the other hand, plastic hanging baskets usually have a drip tray incorporated, which means that not only do you have fewer worries about water falling on other plants or on the heads of people, but a single watering will last

26

longer, for the moisture that collects in this tray is more or less a reservoir for the main basket, the water being released slowly as it is needed.

Useful plants for hanging baskets include several varieties of the ever-popular pelargonium, some of the smaller-leaved ivies, sweet alyssum, lobelia, impatiens, nasturtium, petunia, thunbergia, and some of the begonias. Among the tender perennials choose from *Achimenes*, several of the more pendulous fuchsias, *Hoya bella*, the quick-growing plectranthus with its glossy leaves and some of the tradescantias and zebrinas. And, of course, ferns, both the tender house plant kinds and some hardy species, such as the Christmas fern, are graceful hanging basket subjects for shade.

Left: Line a hanging basket, then fill with a moisture-retentive soil. Allow some plants to trail.

Below: Fix hanging baskets securely and high enough to be out of the way of passers-by.

3 Soils

To the uninitiated, too often soil is just 'dirt', which is a pity because soil is really an active, living material that not only gives the plant support, but provides the means by which life is sustained.

Soils differ widely in their ability to sustain plant life. Because of their physical and chemical makeup some plants do well in soils that are inhospitable to others.

Sandy soils, for instance, do not support plants that require large amounts of plant food and water. At the other extreme, soils with heavy clay content will not provide a suitable environment for plants whose roots cannot be continually wet.

Soils that combine low percentages of sand and clay particles, with a high percentage of decayed organic matter are called loams. These soils support a wide variety of plant life and therefore make the best garden soils.

The addition of well-rotted organic matter, such as barnyard manure, peatmoss, or homemade compost, can modify a soil's

Where garden soils are alkaline, it is best to grow broadleaf evergreens, such as rhododendrons and azaleas in large containers filled with a safe and nourishing acid-soil mixture.

A soil test kit determines deficiencies in plant food content. It also determines the acidity or alkalinity of the soil. A sample of soil is mixed with an 'indicator' chemical. The resulting color is compared to a chart.

physical makeup, holding plant food and water in sandy soils, yet, opening up clay soils with their tightly knit structure. Air, water and plant food are allowed to enter the root zone. Excess water is not trapped, but allowed to move into the subsoil.

Soil also has a chemical nature that can affect plants' performance. Obvious is the need for certain plant foods to be made available. Not so clear is the soil's pH. The easiest way to understand this concept is to think of soils measured on a yardstick, with those of an alkaline nature at one end, and those described as acidic being on the other. At the center of the yard stick is the neutral designation.

Most soils are nearly neutral, although some may be on the alkaline side, while others may be somewhat acidic. Most prairie or grassland soils are somewhat alkaline, while those developed under oak and certain conifer forests are probably acidic. Heavy applications of fertilizers over a period of time can also effect pH. However, if soils are being tested for plant food content, a pH test is a wise investment.

Lime is the common material used to bring a somewhat acidic soil back to a neutral position on the yardstick. Sometimes a soil is too alkaline for growing certain plants, such as rhododendron or evergreen azaleas. Aluminum sulfate is then applied to make the necessary correction.

While the preceding explanation is of more value to those who have a plot of ground, rather than gardening in containers, it is good to have an understanding of how soil can affect a plant's performance.

Most of us will plant our hanging baskets, patio tubs and window boxes with a commercial mix, rather than attempting to correct soil from the garden.

First of all, the commercial potting soils provide an ideal physical environment, allowing adequate amounts of plant food and moisture to be held in the root zone, yet providing drainage for excess water. Most potting soils also contain a small amount of fertilizer to get plants off to a fast start.

Because potting soils have been sterilized, these mixes largely prevent the possibility of weed seeds germinating and the spread of disease.

However, if you have a large number of containers to plant, mixing your own potting soil is unavoidable to save money.

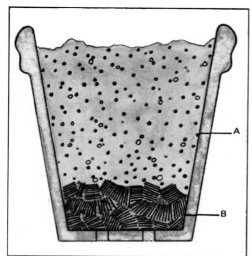

A good layer of drainage material (B) at the base of a pot will help the soil mixture (A) to remain moist without being waterlogged.

imperative that it is kept this way. The activity is carried out by millions of bacteria and enzymes that are continually at work, breaking complex chemical compounds into simple plant foods. These microscopic creatures are kept active and in plentiful supply by humus—organic material composed of rotted leaves, bark, other forms of vegetative and animal waste. This decaying material keeps the soil surface open and the entire soil spectrum breathing.

Because humus is the living part of the soil, it is helpful to keep the humus content high. In some areas, it is possible to buy quantities of farmyard manure. In others, only the processed and bagged manure can be bought. Manures are not only valuable sources of humus, but they also provide plant food value. The amount of plant food available varies between animal classes and what rations were fed. However, some work done recently on the food content of broiler chicken manure in the southern U.S., established that gardeners could depend on this material to yield at least 11 percent nitrogen.

If farmyard material is being considered for use in containers, be sure it is well-rotted, otherwise it is possible that ammonia or other toxic chemicals will burn plant roots.

The first factor to consider is soil texture. Because containers require frequent watering, ordinary garden soils will cake and crust over, preventing air, water and fertilizers to enter the root zone. For this reason organic material, such as peat, garden compost, finely ground bark or dried animal manures must be added.

In addition to aiding soil texture, these materials add plant food to the mix. While peat does not increase soil fertility, much of its value lies in moisture retention capability.

If bark is being used, be certain it is well-rotted. Newly processed bark has been shown to cause a net loss in available nitrogen.

To promote drainage and assist in the even distribution of water, air and plant-food, some sand should also be added to the mixture. However, if a large percentage of bark is being used in the mix, this may not be necessary.

Humus

At the beginning of this chapter soil was described as an active, living material. It is

Making your own compost Humus can also be provided by homemade compost, the result of rotting down almost any kind of vegetable matter. It is worthwhile making your own compost. Not only does it enable you to get rid of vegetable waste in a productive manner, but it saves time and money which otherwise would need to be expended on other forms of organic material. Even the owner of a balcony with a few pots, or a window box gardener can still make compost with little trouble.

If you operate only one or two window boxes, or a few pots on a balcony, then your simplest means of making humus-rich compost is to use as your factory a plain, black plastic bag. Place in it every fallen leaf, every outer leaf of lettuce or cabbage, eggshells, carrot tops, potato peelings, apple cores, and even dust from the vacuum cleaner. Just drop this material in and close the bag again. If the bag is fairly large, add some soil and one of the decomposition agents available at your local garden center. If the soil content appears to remain low, just drop in a spadeful every now and then.

Within two or three months in summer, longer in colder months, all vegetable material will have rotted down to become a rich, dark friable soil-like material. This compost will aid soil texture in your containers and provide some nutritive value. When plants are actively growing, the compost can be spread on the soil surface. Between crops, the organic material can be worked into the soil.

Container gardeners often find the soil level in some of their pots has dropped. A

This compost bin contains layers of decomposing material (C), decomposition accelerator (B) and soil (A). Allow breathing spaces in the sides of the bin, but cover the top to retain warmth and keep out rain.

container which was filled with soil early in the year seems to have much less in it later on. Part of this is settling of soil into the pot. Some soil is washed away during watering and storms, yet wind carries a portion from the surface. This is where your homemade compost can be used to ensure plants remain in good health. Merely add a few trowels full to the soil in each container and let it drift down into the root zone. If you have no homemade compost, top dress your containers once a year with a similar material, such as dried manure, spent hops, or peat. Add a handful of slow-activing fertilizer.

Homemade compost is only a soil amendment and is never to be used alone in containers.

Fertilizer

Plants growing naturally in the soil can send their roots ranging far and wide in search of food and moisture, but a plant growing in a container cannot do this. It is

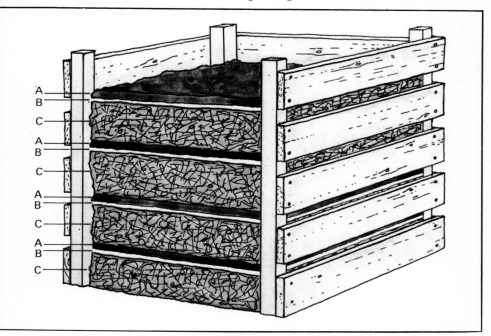

limited to the medium in which it grows and no amount of searching can produce any extra nourishment. The fertilizer existing in a container is quickly lost, for not only is it used by the plant, but it is leached out of the root zone by frequent watering. So, a containerized plant will always require greater attention to feeding than a similar plant growing in the garden.

It is possible to make up your own fertilizers from basic chemicals purchased from a farm supply outlet. This is not very satisfactory, however, because you greatly increase the risk of damaging your plants by fertilizing too heavily. It is much more convenient, and safer, to buy a specialty fertilizer already formulated for container culture.

Alyssum, lobelia and geraniums, all familiar flowers, are growing and performing well because they are fed regularly with a balanced fertilizer.

Granular and liquid forms are available. A granular type is usually applied as a starter in the soil mix before plants are inserted. Liquids are usually applied to maintain plant health throughout the growing season. Ease of application and quick response, without danger of burning, are the major reasons for using a liquid product. Another advantage for liquids is that certain pesticides can be applied at the same time. When using chemical fertilizers, follow directions on bag or bottle with greatest care. Never give your plants just a little extra for luck, because it may kill them. It is far better to make smaller frequent feedings than large ones less often. Measure accurately the amount of material to be applied. It is too easy to take a handful of granular fertilizer and randomly apply it, imagining it is the correct amount, when it could be half or twice the amount actually needed.

4 Techniques

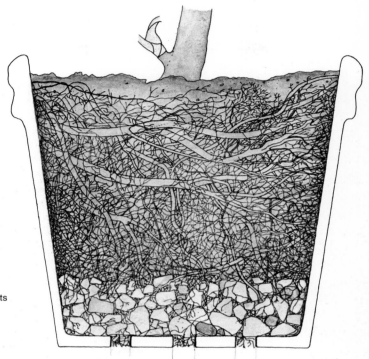

A plant's roots travel round in its container searching always for fresh moisture and fertilizer to keep it in good health.

With few exceptions, plants for patios, window boxes and balconies usually have to be grown in containers. A plant growing in a container can be killed in a day by neglect: it depends entirely on the gardener for its life because it cannot send its roots out in search of food and drink.

The soil in which plants grow is important. But this is not enough, for plants, like humans, need food and moisture, light, air, warmth and a degree of shelter. And the roots have as much need of these benefits as do the branches, foliage and flowers.

Aeration

Plants in containers need more water than plants in the ground, and this will affect the soil. Some of the soil is washed away, the fertilizer content is leached out, the surface may become brick-like, and the drainage holes may become clogged up.

Attention must be paid to the top and bottom of the soil. Scratch the soil surface lightly every now and then to open it up to the air. It also helps to mulch the soil surface once or twice a year with a rich leaf-mold, with a well-rotted farmyard manure, or even with a handful or two of moist peat.

Drainage

The base of the soil in a container cannot be reached, of course, but at the time of initial planting, before the soil is poured in, be

33

sure to include a layer of drainage material such as broken crocks, pebbles, or pea gravel. This will allow moisture to course through the soil quickly and easily. A spongy material, such as coarse peat or well-rotted farmyard manure, placed between the drainage layer and the soil will prevent over-quick drying out of the soil in larger containers.

Light and shade

It is not always easy to provide enough light when growing plants on an enclosed patio, on a shaded balcony, or in a window box on the north side of a building. Most plants will grow, but they cannot be expected to give their best. In some circumstances it may be possible to paint one of the walls in a light color, which will reflect more light. But the important thing is to choose plants that will grow happily and well under conditions of constant shade. It will also help where possible to give the container a quar

Above: Poor light can be considerably improved by painting nearby walls a light color.
Below: If it is impossible to improve the light, grow only plants that tolerate shady conditions.

Roots can be kept at an even temperature by surrounding the plant pot with insulating material.

ter turn once a week or so to ensure that light strikes all sides of the plant, so that it grows upright instead of leaning towards the light. It is sometimes possible to move plants around so that, by rotation, each plant will have a chance of receiving some sunlight.

Temperature

Plants must be selected according to the climate and the situation or aspect in which they will be placed. Many plants like to have their head in the sun and their feet in the shade, and this should not be difficult to arrange. In hot sunshine the heat from the container may be transferred to the soil and then to the roots. To keep the soil cool, small containers can be placed inside larger ones, with the space between filled with dry peat or some other insulating material. Larger containers will have to be protected from the sun by some kind of portable shelter, such as a sun umbrella.

Pests and diseases

Container-grown plants are less open to trouble from pests and diseases than those grown in garden soil. We can quickly and easily clear our plants from any pest infestation with proprietary pesticides. Frequently, it is possible to pick off caterpillars from a plant, or to wash off aphids and red spider mites with soapy water.

Diseases can be brought by insect attack or can be the result of physiological disorder. They are less easy to cure than insect attack, but just as easy to prevent. Any plant susceptible to mildew or other fungal trouble should be sprayed before the disease is apparent, thus keeping it at bay.

Town sparrows can cause damage to town-grown plants, especially as they love to take dust baths in beds of fine soil sown with seeds. Large areas can have black thread strung over them, just 2–4 in (5–10 cm) above the soil. Small plants can be protected with a temporary dome of wire netting, and the sparrows can be kept off some plants by spraying or dusting the plants with one of the modern deterrents.

A wire netting dome can easily and quickly be slipped over a plant if it is being attacked by birds.

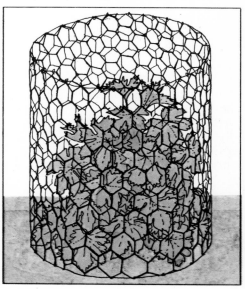

5 Roof gardens

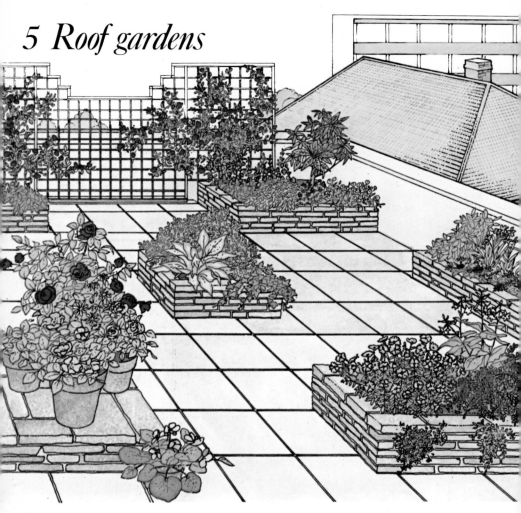

The main advantage of a roof garden over other forms of gardening above ground level is one of sheer space. On a roof the sky is literally the limit – at least in one dimension, and other boundaries depend on the size of the building. Yet all plants will have to be grown in some container, which means watering will be a constant exercise. Winds can be a problem on a roof, but shade will probably cause less trouble.

Preparation

Before beginning any roof garden it is vital that the actual roof surface be examined to

Rich soil and copious watering will result in lush growth on the roof garden, and this in turn will help to keep the roots always cool and moist.

make quite sure that it cannot be damaged. The structure of the building should also be investigated because if the garden is to be extensive in any way, the extra weight that will be placed on the load-bearing sections may be very considerable. When it is wet, soil can be very heavy indeed. Where the roof is composed of some bituminous material, take care that all containers placed on it have rounded edges, rather than sharp ones, for sharp edges can easily work into

36

sun-softened bitumen and can cut and pierce it.

On some roofs it is possible to make beds around the circumference by containing soil with bricks. Most roofs have a low retaining wall around them for safety reasons and soil can be placed against this wall and held in position by the bricks. Here it is especially necessary to make quite certain that the roof surface is sound and, in particular, that the junction of roof and wall is free from any cracks or faults. The roots of plants will easily find their way into any crevice or crack and quickly enlarge the opening until water can seep through and cause damage.

Beds of this type present the greatest opportunities for effective roof gardening. One advantage is that with complete beds, all plant roots will have a wider area in which to roam. Also, the soil will take longer to dry out, so watering will be less of a problem. And because it is possible to

The larger the size of the bed on a roof garden, the greater the moisture reservoir there will be and the less watering that will be necessary.

37

have a greater depth of soil, taller trees can be grown without the danger that they will be blown over. Aesthetically, it is more satisfying to grow plants in a long and comparatively wide bed than in a series of small containers.

It is possible, too, to install special soils for special plants. Azaleas, which require an acid soil, grow well on rooftops, and so do various pinks and carnations, which prefer a more alkaline mixture. It would be unwise to try to grow bog plants on a roof, but the location admirably suits the drier and sandier soils demanded by cacti and other succulents. Herbs for the kitchen can quite easily be grown, as well as an occasional lettuce, some radishes and perhaps even some carrots. If there is space to spare, it is quite possible to grow pots of tomatoes, so long as you can find a place for them that is protected from strong winds.

Left: Carnations like a mildly alkaline soil mixture, easily provided in a container on a roof.

Below: Cacti and other succulents grow well on a roof because there they get the hot sunshine they need.

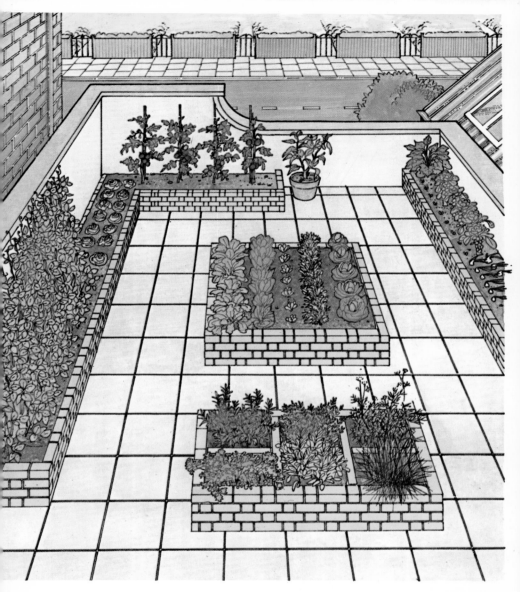

Watering

The greatest problem on a roof garden, as with gardening on a balcony or in a window box, is watering. Whether plants are being grown in containers or in artificial beds, neither has any quantity or depth of soil, which means that evaporation in the sun and air is quick. Watering must be thorough and frequent, sometimes twice a

If attention is paid to their watering, vegetables and herbs will grow well and quickly on a roof. When you are harvesting your crops, make sure all city dust and grime are washed away.

day. Not all roof gardens have facilities for such frequent watering, but with a little ingenuity it is usually possible to rig up a hosepipe from some convenient spot on the floor below and lead this onto the roof.

Take care when watering that gusts of wind do not send showers into open windows nearby or onto the streets below. Make sure also that all drainage pipes are kept free of fallen leaves or other debris that might block them and cause trouble.

Other roof garden features

Every roof garden should provide space for leisure. Arrange plantings so that at the hottest part of the day the leisure area is in shade. A strategically placed tree or a vine-covered pergola, both perfectly possible on a large roof, can provide shade and add interest to the area.

Some roof gardens have space for a small greenhouse. These are especially useful for the raising of seedlings and for the restoration of ailing house plants. Failing a greenhouse, it is almost always possible to install a frame or even a Hotkap in which to bring on seedlings or protect tender plants.

All gardening produces waste vegetable matter. This can be converted into soil or compost and stored in a roof garden. With the necessary care, rooftop gardening, like other kinds of gardening in containers, can offer new and rewarding possibilities.

A roof garden is an ideal place for a small greenhouse.

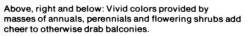

Above, right and below: Vivid colors provided by masses of annuals, perennials and flowering shrubs add cheer to otherwise drab balconies.

Above: Cascading fuchsias make useful, decorative plants. Below: This brilliant display is composed primarily of begonias and geraniums. Above right:

Verbena and heliotrope, with large violet-blue clusters, make a bright splash of color on this patio.

There are a lot of hybrid Japanese maples, many of them dwarf and suited to tub culture, and all particularly attractive because of the shape and color of the rich foliage.

The right plant for the right container

Any plant that will grow in the soil will grow in a container. Surprisingly large trees and shrubs will grow in comparatively small containers, but not for long. It is wise to try to match the size of the plant with the size of the container. Bear in mind the fact that the roots of a plant are roughly the same size as that part of a plant that grows above ground. A tree's roots will extend more or less to the same area as that occupied by the branches. This means that in a tub or pot the roots must coil round and

round, and this indeed they do until they just cannot grow any longer or find any more space open to them. They will then sometimes break the container, but more often they will begin to die.

However, really large trees or shrubs do not look right except in a container so large that it is fitted for a park, stately home or town square rather than the confined patio. Because so large a container cannot be fitted into limited space, we might be tempted to employ a smaller but lightweight container and here we will again run into trouble, for it will be found that the least puff of wind will overbalance the tree and send it over on its side. A large tree or shrub will also require staking. Not only do stakes take away from the plant's beauty, but they are difficult to fix firmly in place.

Because any container plant attracts more attention than a comparable one growing in a bed or border, it should be an evergreen. A winter skeleton in a tub is not an attractive object. The only exceptions are deciduous shrubs of interesting branching habit such as *Corylus avellana 'contorta'*.

The roots of an azalea must always be kept moist, so use a peaty, water-absorbent soil mixture.

Sometimes, the effect you may wish container planting to achieve is not possible with anything other than natural materials

This is particularly true if you are tired of planting herbaceous flowering varieties in one dimensional hanging baskets.

If you wish to experiment, staple chicken wire to a piece of driftwood or forest down fall, to form graceful planting pockets. The chicken wire can be lined with dampened strips of sphagnum peat moss, followed by potting soil and selected plants.

A screw-in hook and chain will support your new natural planter from a roof overhang. Remember to soak ocean driftwood for several days in a pail of water to remove salt.

Above: Choisya ternata, a hardy evergreen shrub with aromatic foliage and sweetly scented flowers, enjoys some shelter from a wall.

Right: Where a formal shape is required, most evergreens will respond to gradual and gentle clipping and training given two or three times a year.

Plants for the patio Some of the most useful plants for the patio are those that cover a considerable area yet leave the limited floor space almost entirely free – climbers. They take up little space yet give a vast return in providing leaves and sometimes flowers in abundance. They soften outlines, blur sharp angles and help to bring peace and quiet.

The most useful climbers are those that are both evergreen and self-clinging, but, unfortunately, there are only a few of these, especially in the North. Probably the best is the ivy, available in a wide range of varieties, colors and leaf sizes. The ivy will cling to a wall yet do little or no damage to it except after many years. It will make no demands in the way of special feeding or watering so long as it is growing in the soil and not in a pot. It can quite easily be trained to travel in any direction you choose and is quite simple to prune.

Among some of the other evergreen climbers there is *Eccremocarpus scaber*, the Chilean glorybower, with attractive fern-like foliage and, in the summer, orange-red tubular flowers, followed by unusual seed pods shaped like a small sack or bladder. This vine is only winter-hardy and evergreen in the south. Elsewhere it can be grown as an annual, but seeds must be started early indoors.

Berberidopsis corallina, the coral plant, has dark green, heart-shaped leaves, their undersides a glaucous blue-gray. It pro-

Useful because it flowers in winter, *Erica carnea* has many varieties with colored flowers and foliage.

vides pendulous clusters of dark red flowers in summer.

Shrubs that are grown on the patio will have to be fairly small, whether they are grown in the soil or in a container. This is just as well, for if any shrub is to be grown in a space where its roots have little room to travel, it will tend to stay rather smaller than if given plenty of space. Although dwarfed to a certain extent by the environment, there is no reason why most suitable shrubs should not live for some years.

Once again evergreens are useful because they are decorative at all times of the year. One that has several uses is the sweet bay, *Laurus nobilis*, which can be pruned into shape so that it becomes living sculpture. It also provides the occasional leaf for the kitchen pot when needed. It will grow in sun or shade, but in Northern regions must be grown in a tub so it can be brought indoors over winter.

Another evergreen that will stand shaping is the common box, *Buxus sempervirens*. Hardier in the North are the varieties of Korean box (*B. microphylla koreana*). These will grow in sun or shade.

If there is space for two or more plants of aucuba, you can have small, tough, evergreen shrubs that will grow in sun or shade and in grossly polluted air, and at the same time will provide glossy green and gold leaves and shining red berries. Aucuba is winter-hardy where temperatures don't fall much below 10°F (22°C).

There are a considerable number of deciduous or evergreen cotoneasters that will do well in soil or in containers on the patio, most of them bearing white flowers to be followed by scarlet berries, the flowers loved by bees and the berries by birds. Many of the cotoneasters are shrubs, some can be trees and there are others that either can be prostrate or will lean happily against a wall almost like a climber.

Two evergreen species of the normally deciduous euonymus, or the spindle, are *E. fortunei* and *E. japonica*, both with a number of varieties with differing leaf shape, size and color. Both of these are tolerant of soil, sun or shade.

Fatsia japonica makes an excellent pot plant, producing large distinctive palmate leaves.

Ruta graveolens 'Jackman's Blue' is a variety with a low compact habit of growth and bright blue-grey foliage.

An exceptionally hardy evergreen holly is inkberry, Il ex glabra, which bears black berries. This shrub of medium height is tolerant of city conditions and will grow in partial shade.

And, finally, consider the glorious pieris, hardy evergreens with the most dainty appearance. *Pieris forrestii* and *P. taiwanensis* are two species that come immediately to mind, but there are several more and a number of useful varieties. Some of these produce pretty racemes of little white flowers like lily-of-the-valley and are noted also for their young springtime growth of vivid scarlet shoots. The pieris like a moist and peaty soil together with a lightly shaded position.

Trees and shrubs

In the next few pages a number of trees and shrubs are briefly examined, most of them evergreen because they remain attractive even in winter months. It is suggested that, except under the most favorable circumstances, they are suitable only for growing on a patio or roof garden. They are too large for all but the most magnificent balcony and of course unsuited to a window

box. Plants suited to these sites will be discussed in detail later. Because of the varying hardiness of these shrubs and trees, check with your local garden center to see whether a proposed container plant will survive winters in your area.

Although deciduous, some of the dwarf Japanese maples make first class patio plants. Often gnarled and twisted, they appear almost like bonsai and the vivid colors of their leaves attract immediate attention. *Acer palmatum 'atropurpureum'* is thickly covered with small wine-red maple shaped leaves. The red cutleaf form has a graceful habit, with branches cascading from a short, thick trunk.

A good broadleaf evergreen that will grow in sun or shade, in dry or moist soils, in city or country, is *Aucuba japonica*, available in several forms large and small, with white, yellow or red berries. Depending on

The bright lemon-yellow flowers of *Santolina chamaecyparissus*, or cotton lavender, contrast with the silvery, woolly foliage.

Camellias require an acid soil if they are to flourish, which is easily provided in a tub.

variety chosen, foliage can be green or with interesting gold variegation. You must have bushes of both sexes to get berries. Although this shrub will tolerate occasional freezing temperatures, it will not survive hard, prolonged winters.

If you have space and are prepared to spend time looking for varieties that are harmonious with your patio decor, investigate Japanese varieties of evergreen azaleas. These low-growing, flat-topped shrubs produce masses of blooms in late spring and early summer ranging from pink, red and yellow tones. Azaleas need a moist, peaty soil and a situation that is protected from strong sunlight and wind.

Boxwood is another broadleaf evergreen of more reliable hardiness. One of its main attributes is that it can be trained to nearly any shape and kept to a size desirable for container planting. *Buxus sempervirens* is the most popular variety, with small glossy green leaves. Variegated leaf forms are also available.

Starry-white flowers are produced in May on plants of *Choisya ternata*, or Mexican Orange. This robust shrub will grow nearly

6½ ft. and again, it is easily trained. Glossy leaves and the orange-scented flowers combine to make this a good patio plant, but only in the southern U.S. and California.

There are a number of cotoneasters, both deciduous and broadleaf evergreen, which grow well in containers and which not only give masses of little flowers in the spring but follow these with berries, usually scarlet. Bees love the blooms and birds the berries. There are many cotoneasters, both evergreen kinds for less severe climates and deciduous ones for more rugged regions that can be in the form of trees, shrubs or sprawling plants. Most can be trained to grow as you want them.

Most ericas or heathers must have a lime-free soil in which to grow, but this is not so with *Erica carnea*. Nevertheless, with container-grown plants, it is easy enough to tailor the soil to the plant, so ericas should be attended to very closely because so many of them will give excellent winter color.

A splendid architectural plant for the patio is *Fatsia japonica*, bearing large, dramatic, glossy green, palmate leaves. The flowers are insignificant and even the berries are subordinate to the foliage. Fat-

Never use shears to prune *Laurus nobilis*, the bay tree. Use secateurs or scissors to cut away whole leaves.

The vivid scarlet berries of *Pyracantha coccinea* show at their best against a wall. Not strictly a climber because the plant needs support, the pyracantha responds well to training.

sia and the bay tree that follows are good container plants in the North, where they are not winter-hardy. Plants in tubs can be brought indoors to a sun porch or well-lighted but cool room until spring.

Culinary bay leaves are picked from plants of the sweet bay, *Laurus nobilis*, which is also decorative and useful. It is not a spectacular plant and is best grown clipped or pinched to familiar and formal shape. It will grow in sun or shade, and it is an evergreen.

Another subshrub, and barely evergreen in the North with a pearly-gray foliage, is the medicinal herb rue, *Ruta graveolens*. Keep the shrub trimmed back each spring and concentrate on getting good foliage by removing the yellow flowers, which begin to appear in the early summer, before they open.

Santolina is yet another silver, gray or almost white-leaved bush that will benefit from being cut back in the early spring, almost to the previous year's growth. The best form is *Santolina chamaecyparissus*, small, thick growing and producing masses of yel-

low flowers in midsummer. Remove these flowers as they pass their best and you will achieve a constant succession almost all summer through.

There are so many hardy conifers suitable for containers and patios. They have great architectural value with their formal shapes: they can be upright, conical or low and spreading; they can be green, glaucous blue, gold or silver. They are easy, tolerant plants to grow so long as they are not allowed to become dry at their roots. There are dwarf and slow-growing varieties of conifer that will live for many years in a large pot. A golden conifer in the wintertime can be just as bright as a tree of flowers.

One of the slowest-growing conifers is the dwarf Alberta spruce (*Picea glauca* 'Conica'), which maintains a perfect cone shape year after year. At the other extreme in shape is the mugo pine (*Pinus mugo*), which in some choice forms grows like a pincushion.

If you are in doubt about the most suitable conifers for tubs and for your locality,

Top: The young foliage of *Pieris forrestii* is a vivid red, even outshining the little white flowers.
Above: Euonymus fortunei, the spindle, has several forms, green or variegated prostrate or upright.

consult your local nursery. They will have a wide knowledge of the best conifers for you. Conifers that grow too large for their containers can be a total disaster.

There are some good container possibilities among the evergreen barberries. Consider the warty barberry (*Berberis verruculosa*), which has spiny, lustrous leaves that are white on their undersides. In fall the foliage takes on bronze tints. Among the evergreen privets are the Japanese (*Ligustrum japonicum*) and glossy (*L. lucidum*), both much grown in the South, but usually winter-hardy as far as Long Island.

An interesting deciduous shrub that is very hardy and that can be grown in a tub for a time is the winged euonymus (*E. alatus*). Its winter form is very sculptural.

Bonsai trees

Not suited to growing in a window box, but almost tailored to a life on balcony or patio are examples of the ancient Japanese art of bonsai, the art of dwarfing trees. Although

bonsai trees are sometimes thought of as indoor subjects, they are just as much outdoor trees as their fully-grown brothers. They can be brought indoors for brief periods to be enjoyed in the comfort of the home, but must be taken out again in a day or two, for the home is normally too hot and dry for them.

And even outdoors they must receive some protection against the elements. They must not, for example, be placed where the sun will be on them for more than a short period each day, for their root system is short and shallow. Even if the handful of soil around the roots is kept moist, this moisture cannot be taken up to the leafy extremities at the pace necessitated by the warmth of the sun. They must also be placed in a position where they do not stand in a strong wind. This can knock them over, break their sometimes frail leaves and once again lead to transpiration at a rate that cannot be compensated by the dwarf and delicate root system.

However, if you enjoy bonsai trees and wish to grow them on the patio or the bal-

The container is as important as the tree in creating a beautiful bonsai specimen, and the two should therefore be selected to harmonize with each other.

cony and can give them the necessary elementary protection, the following notes may be of assistance.

There are four basic ways of starting a bonsai collection, and in order of descending expense these are as follows. At the top is the purchase of genuine, old, trained examples of bonsai already planted in suitable containers. This can be a very expensive matter indeed and, unless you have some basic experience of handling these miniatures, it would seem to be unwise. But, on the other hand, the basic training work will have been completed and your tasks will simply be of maintenance. Any reputable dealer will guarantee your trees, give you advice and assistance, and some will take your tree annually for what could almost be called servicing.

It is often a good idea, by the way, to have this servicing carried out when you intend to take your vacations. Often, at such times, it is a worry to leave treasured

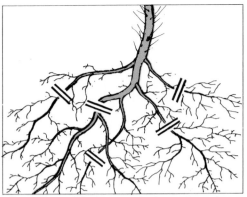

Above: Some of the heavy anchoring roots can be pruned away to save space in the bonsai container.

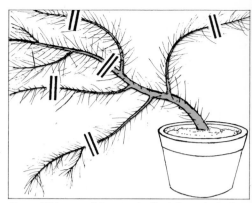

Above: With a careful eye to the final shape desired, cut away some of the excess stem growth.

plants with inexperienced people.

Next in order comes the purchase of trees some five to ten years of age, with a certain minimum of training already given to them. They will have been dwarfed and root pruned several times and their basic shape will have been decided and will be apparent. These trees will be comparatively inexpensive, although the price will reflect the work that has been carried out on them. They may or may not be planted in a decorative container, and may be growing in a flower pot and it will be up to the new owner to transplant them and to grow them on. Look for healthy growth with no signs of disease, damage or insect attack. Make quite sure that you see and understand the purpose and the shape of the preliminary shaping and training that have been done. See that any cuts made were cleanly done, without snags or shredding. Check that the soil in which the plant is growing is moist, yet aerated and well-drained, that no roots protrude above soil level and that the tree is held firm without any trace of rocking. If training wire is wound around branches, see that it is fulfilling its purpose without cutting into the surface.

Buy your container at the same time, making quite sure to choose one that the young tree will be able to grow in for many years and that conforms to the tree in shape as well as size.

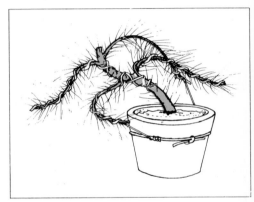

Above: Use soft copper wire to bend and control the line of the branches, but never make this too tight.

You can buy young trees through the mail from specialist nurseries for suspiciously low prices, and by doing so you may waste your money. They are inexpensive because they are usually seedlings and are weak, quite incapable of traveling and being brought up in a completely different atmosphere.

If you wish to start from the beginning, it is much better to find and grow on your own trees. Any gardener will know that young oak trees, maples, pines and one or two others are constantly appearing in flower beds as the result of bird, mouse or squirrel activity. If these are carefully dug up, potted, cared for and gradually trained, they are likely to grow into something which is both useful and attractive and which will give you pleasure.

The training of the bonsai tree consists of a somewhat complex balance of maintaining good growth and pinching out growing tips, of bending and splinting to shape, of pruning roots to keep them small in bulk yet capable of feeding the plant with the necessary food and moisture. Although the process could not be described as difficult, a certain talent and a certain sensitivity are necessary in order to obtain really good results with bonsai.

Flowering and foliage plants

The world of herbaceous plants (annuals and perennials) suitable for growing in containers on the patio, on the balcony and even in certain window boxes is a huge one, but it is necessary to be selective. In the first place one must turn down any plants that will grow very tall or will fall and flop about unless they are disciplined and staked. Secondly, one does not wish to make use of plants with so brief a life that they constantly need replacing. This can be the case with a number of herbaceous favorites if they do not get enough moisture at their roots. In general, it will be found that it is best to stick to just a few kinds. Too many plants of too many colors can tire the eye and give a restless, hot and over-busy appearance.

The following list comprises suggestions for plants that can be grown on the patio,

An old bonsai specimen makes a good patio plant.

on the balcony or, in many cases, in window boxes. The average growing height is given for each and there are occasional comments and suggestions. It is impossible to cope here with every combination of conditions that might be met and for this reason it is probable that certain varieties or species will not be successful in certain places. Little will be lost. Experiment will be helpful because it will reveal sometimes surprising results. Although some species or varieties will be suitable, others will not, and a choice must be made.

Ageratum

Names	Measurement	Comments
Achillea	10–20 in (25–50 cm)	Choose dwarf forms of this early summer-blooming perennial.
Achimenes	1–2 ft (30–60 cm)	Tender perennial grown from tiny tubers. Wide range of pink through purple flowers all summer. A trailer for baskets or window boxes.
Ageratum houstonianum	4–20 in (10–50 cm)	Annual that blooms and blooms.
Ajuga bugle	5–15 in (12–36 cm)	Perennial ground cover with blue flowers in spring. Will clothe a large tub.
Alyssum (syn. **Lobularia**) **maritima**	4–6 in (10–15 cm)	Hackneyed, perhaps, but easy from seed and excellent for carpeting, for odd corners and boxes. Fragrant.
Antirrhinum majus snapdragon	7–50 in (18–125 cm)	Tender perennial. Use dwarf varieties, such as 'Floral Carpet', for containers.

Asperula

Begonia

Antirrhinum   *Armeria*

Names	Measurement	Comments
Arabis rock cress	6–10 in (15–25 cm)	A perennial that may take over a tub or window box, but only spring-blooming.
Armeria thrift	2–13 in (5–45 cm)	Perennials with flowers of long and lasting life in early summer. Needs full sun and good drainage.
Asperula odorata sweet woodruff	8 in (20 cm)	Dainty-leaved groundcover for partial shade. Perennial.
Begonia		Wide range of shapes, sizes and colors. Among the best for containers and patio decoration.
Bellis perennis English daisy	6 in (15 cm)	Annual or biennial, blooming from spring to early summer.
Campanula bellflower	10–60 in (25–150 cm)	A wide choice, but rock garden types best, except for temporary effects possible from Canterbury bells. Grow *C. isophylla* (Italian bellflower) in hanging baskets.

Bellis   *Campanula*

Cheiranthus

Chrysanthemum

Names	Measurement	Comments
Cheiranthus wallflower	10–20 in (25–50 cm)	Dwarf and colorful. Spring flowers only.
Chrysanthemum	12–24 in (30–60 cm)	Wide choice of types and varieties, all long-lasting. Late summer-autumn.
Coleus blumei	8–24 in (20–60 cm)	Tender perennial, easy from seeds and cuttings. Varicolored foliage.
Dahlia, Dwarf	10–24 in (25–60 cm)	Tender tuberous perennial. Dwarf types bloom from early summer to frost, and are excellent in tubs.
Dianthus	6–20 in (15–50 cm)	Many sweet-smelling pinks that will do well as long as they have good sun and well-drained soil.
Eschscholzia californica California poppy	24 in (60 cm)	Seeds must be sown in early spring or fall during cool weather. Then needs full sun and good drainage.

Gaillardia

Iberis

Dianthus

Eschscholzia

Names	Measurement	Comments
Fuchsia	3–5 ft (90–150 cm)	Tender shrubs, almost solely pot and tub subjects in the North. Procumbent types fine in hanging baskets in partial shade.
Gaillardia	18–36 in (45–90 cm)	Perennial needing full sun and good drainage. Summer-blooming.
Heliotropium arborescens heliotrope	2–6 ft (60–180 cm)	Tender shrub long popular for baskets, as standards in tubs or for bedding around a patio, where its fragrant purple flowers can be enjoyed.
Hemerocallis day-lily	24–72 in (60–180 cm)	Choose the lower growing varieties of strong fragrance for tubs on a patio.
Iberis sempervirens candytuft	10–20 in (25–50 cm)	Several useful evergreen varieties with mostly spring flowers. Require full sun and good drainage. Plant around the edges of raised beds.

Impatiens

Lysimachia

Pelargonium

Petunia

Names	Measurement	Comments
Impatiens wallerana patience-plant	12–24 in (30–60 cm)	Popular indoors as well as out in its many new varieties. A tender perennial easy from seeds and cuttings. Fine in hanging baskets, boxes or in ground beds around patio. Endures semi-shade.
Lysimachia nummularia moneywort, creeping Charlie	1–2 in (3–6 cm)	Perennial trailer that can be weedy in lawns but is safe if confined to a pot. Glossy foliage and yellow flowers all summer.
Pelargonium geranium		Variable height according to how the plant is grown. This is perhaps the best-known and most used container plant in many parts of the world. It is also one of the best.
Petunia	9–24 in (23–60 cm)	Many types, many sizes, many colors, all of them good.

Sedum

Sempervivum

Phlox drummondii

Saxifraga

Names	Measurement	Comments
Phlox drummondii	6–15 in (15–40 cm)	The annual phlox provides a wide and useful range of plants for many locations.
Saxifraga saxifrage	6–12 in (15–30 cm)	There are many kinds and many colors.
Sedum stonecrop	2–8 in (5–20 cm)	Stonecrops of many kinds, shapes, textures and colors are natural inhabitants of troughs and tubs. They are tolerant of neglect.
Sempervivum houseleek	4–12 in (10–30 cm)	Sometimes difficult to differentiate from the stonecrops.
Thymus thyme	2–8 in (5–20 cm)	There are a large number of thymes, mainly creeping or mat-forming, most in vivid colors and all easy to grow.
Viola pansy and viola	4–8 in (10–20 cm)	The biennial pansy is a worthy plant for window boxes and planters in spring.

Thymus

Viola

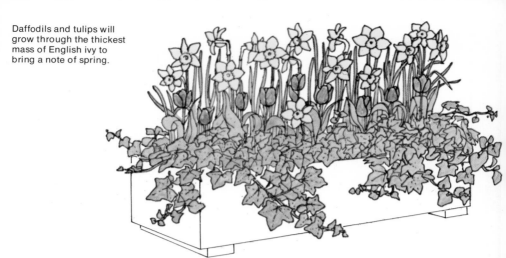

Daffodils and tulips will grow through the thickest mass of English ivy to bring a note of spring.

Plants for window boxes

Some of the preceding plants will grow well in a window box, but circumstances vary here and it is difficult to make recommendations without knowing details. Sun and shade, wind, size of box and depth of soil, all these and other matters affect what plants can most successfully be grown. There is also the personality and the courage of the owner to be taken into account, for some growers will attempt anything and will frequently succeed, whereas others will grow only the tried and tested plants and even then will fail. Window boxes are always tricky because their situation makes them liable to freak winds in some locations, which can either break and batter the plants or can sear them and burn them so that they either die or at the best fail to grow as they otherwise could.

In winter, window boxes can be planted with winter heaths (*Erica*), with the broadleaved green of skimmia, with ivy and some of the dwarf conifers. These will not give much color other than a pleasant green and they will have to be washed or hosed down every so often to remove from the foliage the gritty dust that is almost certain to settle on them if they are being grown in a city. They will, nevertheless, be growing plants and they will be evidence that life still exists in a cold and bleak world.

Before installing your winter plants anticipate spring by underplanting with bulbs. Snowdrops, crocuses, daffodils, tulips and others will grow quite successfully in window boxes, and as they appear, the drab winter occupants can be removed

Below: Petunias are excellent window-box flowers so long as faded flowers are constantly removed.

or allowed to stay with the green leaves of the bulbs growing through them. When choosing your bulbs, make sure you select only the dwarf kinds. Do not attempt to grow any daffodils or tulips with long stems in a window box, for they will almost inevitably snap in the strong winds.

As the bulbs die, so the fear of frost becomes less and when all danger of this has passed, you can prepare for the glory of summer. Trite and commonplace they may be, but the magnificent, easy and showy pelargoniums, or geraniums, take a lot of beating and will last the whole of the summer until the frosts come again. There is the widest possible choice of color, shape and form, including some of the fancy-leaved types that look so well when seen at close range and have aromatic foliage.

If the site is sunny and the soil can be watered frequently, you will find that dwarf zinnias and dwarf or French marigolds will flourish. Petunias will grow colorful and

Above: Clematis can make a good foil for a window box, if correctly trained around the window. *Below*: Geraniums will grow well almost anywhere.

lush if you feed and water them well. Lobelia, sweet alyssum, verbena and the new strong, dwarf and rust-free varieties of antirrhinum will all remain in constant bloom.

Where the boxes are on the shady side of the house, you will probably have more success with wax begonias and impatiens, all of which will give you tremendous amounts of color.

If you are both keen and ambitious, as well as willing to take a chance against the elements, it is quite possible in many circumstances to grow one or two climbers to surround the window frame, particularly the quick-growing climbers and trailers of the tropaeolum family, which gives us

Lobelia, geraniums, petunias, tagetes, alyssum, and begonias all in a container of some kind, are centered round the window box to make a vivid display.

canary creeper and the nasturtiums. Make sure that supports are available and that the tendrils are secured at all times, for it only needs a single long trailer to break free and the whole plant will be in peril from the winds.

If you are not concerned about the view from the window or even the light that enters, it is perfectly possible to grow in the window box a series of climbers that will cover the entire space. A number of examples have been seen of pole beans that have been grown mainly to conceal the view of the house next door, and have also presented the growers with several meals of vegetables. In a case such as this, make sure that supports are firm, that the plants are secure in their growth and that you can get at them for attention and for picking without damage to the plants or danger to you.

Tomatoes in window boxes or small containers require watering two or three times a day in hot weather.

Food crops

It is perfectly possible to grow certain of the smaller food crops, mainly salads, in a window box. Lettuce, radishes, and carrots are examples of this, and certainly strawberries can be grown. If the appearance of the window box is of major concern, then these crops can be grown between flowering plants or, if there is space enough, they can be grown at the back (i.e., the window side) of the box. It is not suggested that any major contribution towards feeding the family can be made by this means, but it is always pleasant to have a freshly cut lettuce plant or crisp radishes straight from the soil.

The secret of all vegetable-growing is to hurry the plants along, grow them quickly, for they are then tender and succulent. To do this it is necessary to have a richer than ordinary soil and plenty of moisture, so incorporate plenty of humus-making material in your soil mixture and use frequent liquid feeds.

Little more can be grown on most balconies than one can raise in a window box, but a patio is a different matter and here, depending on size and inclination, it is possible to have one or two fruit trees, a miniature vegetable patch, a herb garden and other culinary crops.

63

Index